WOULD YOU

Festive

- By Clint Hammerstrike

About the Author

Someone with plenty of free time to write this book and enough imagination to create the name Clint Hammerstrike – seriously why wouldn't you!

What else is there to say other than you will be pleased to know this isn't my day job!

Introduction

Writing this book has been one of the merriest things that I have ever done –what can I say. Clint loves him some festivities! I take great joy in pondering random scenarios and questions. If I was given a sprout for every time I contemplated the questions would I rather X OR Y, I would have enough sprouts to bury a medium sized elephant.

I wrote this book to share with you some of the great festive conundrums we face over the holiday season:

The great thing about this edition is that you not only get to ponder the complexity and bask in the pure joy of each hypothetical but you get to answer by drawing your favored choice!

Remember all of these scenarios are for hypothetical entertainment and drawing purposes and should not be taken as a recommendation or an endorsement. You should never eat a bauble a mince pie full of Santa's beard or Rudolph. Did I really need to say that last one!?!

Helpful Guide

To aid you on this journey of self-discovery I have suggested a couple of rules to help you through.

Rule 1: You must answer. Even if you would rather do neither you MUST pick!

Rule 2: Don't rush your answer. Give yourself time to consider the sheer complexity and horror/joy of the choice!

Rule 3: Respect the opinion of those reading with you? Even when they are plainly wrong!

Rule 4: Take this seriously, we are considering the meaning of life do not even consider laughing!

Rule 5: Forget rule 4. Laugh, come on its dancing with eating a turkey basted in Marmite OR Sherbet!

Rule 6: Draw whatever it is that you have chosen as your favoured option. How you decide to do this is up to you. Be as creative and detailed as you want. Send your best picture to clinthammerstrike@gmail.com and you could feature in a future edition! Alternatively share it online at:
facebook.com/ClintHammerstrike

Let's get drawing

WOULD YOU RATHER:
Drink 5 pints of blended brussel sprouts juice
OR eat an entire turkey suitable for a family of
10?

WOULD YOU RATHER:
Eat a turkey basted in marmite OR sherbet?

WOULD YOU RATHER:
Eat a sausage encased in a Mars Bar OR wrapped in strawberry laces?

WOULD YOU RATHER:
Have your whole Christmas meal blended into a smoothie that taste great OR eat a full dinner but not get all the flavours?

•

WOULD YOU RATHER:
Have to eat a full Christmas dinner every day
of the year OR never eat it again?

WOULD YOU RATHER:
Eat a deep fried Christmas pudding OR deep fried mince pie?

WOULD YOU RATHER:
Eat a reindeer OR an elf?

WOULD YOU RATHER:
Eat a large bauble OR one meter of tinsel?

WOULD YOU RATHER:
Eat a mince pie covered in mayonnaise OR mustard?

WOULD YOU RATHER:
Have to personally kill the turkey you eat OR be vegetarian for Christmas?

WOULD YOU RATHER:
Be told by your doctor that over the Christmas period you couldn't eat anything sweet OR anything savory?

WOULD YOU RATHER:
Eat the contents of a Christmas stocking full of feta cheese and sprouts that has been left by the fire overnight OR drink cranberry sauce out of the boot of a Santa impersonator?

WOULD YOU RATHER:
Eat Dasher, Dancer, Prancer, Vixen, Comet, Cupid, Donner, Blixen OR Rudolph?

WOULD YOU RATHER:
Have to survive the month of December
eating only Quality Streets and Celebrations
OR Roses and Cadbury Heroes?

WOULD YOU RATHER:
Eat a mince pie full of Santa's beard OR holly leaves?

WOULD YOU RATHER:
Try and carve a turkey with a rolling pin OR
a string of fairy lights?

WOULD YOU RATHER:
Have Christmas without alcohol OR any desserts?

WOULD YOU RATHER:
For breakfast eat a bowl of brussel sprouts with milk OR eat a bowl of mince pies with gravy?

WOULD YOU RATHER:
Eat your body weight in Christmas cake OR
yule log?

WOULD YOU RATHER:
For 25 days eat a chocolate covered wasp OR
a chocolate covered slug?

WOULD YOU RATHER:
Have a bowl of gravy poured in your lap OR
be slapped in the face five times with a honey
roasted ham?

WOULD YOU RATHER:
Have a roast dinner OR a barbecue for
Christmas dinner?

WOULD YOU RATHER:
Cook Christmas dinner for Donald Trump OR the Grinch?

WOULD YOU RATHER:
Cook Christmas dinner for David Beckham OR Brad Pitt?

WOULD YOU RATHER:
Cook Christmas dinner for Winnie the Pooh OR Paddington Bear?

WOULD YOU RATHER:
Cook Christmas dinner for Arnold Schwarzenegger OR Sylvester Stallone?

WOULD YOU RATHER:
Cook Christmas dinner for Mark Zuckerberg OR Bill Gates?

WOULD YOU RATHER:
Cook Christmas dinner for Jennifer Lawrence OR Emma Stone?

WOULD YOU RATHER:
Be given a dictionary OR a paperweight as a present?

WOULD YOU RATHER:
Be given socks OR a tie as a present?

WOULD YOU RATHER:
Be given a sports car OR a yacht as a present?

WOULD YOU RATHER:
Be given a unicorn OR a dragon as a present?

WOULD YOU RATHER:
Be given a pair of old pants OR a used toothbrush as a present?

WOULD YOU RATHER:
Be given a quadbike OR a jet ski as a present?

WOULD YOU RATHER:
Be given a rattlesnake OR a tarantula as a present?

WOULD YOU RATHER:
Be given a cheque for £1 million OR a genie
lamp that grants one wish (but not cash) as a
present?

WOULD YOU RATHER:
Be given a bag of toenail clippings OR a bag of hair from a shower drain as a present?

WOULD YOU RATHER:
Be given a fedora that makes you irresistible to Alpaca's OR a trilby that makes birds hate you as a present?

WOULD YOU RATHER:
Be given a lifetime supply of ground cumin
OR athletes foot powder as a present?

WOULD YOU RATHER:
Be given a parrot that says rude things about you OR a gerbil that plots to kill you as a present?

WOULD YOU RATHER:
Be given individually chosen gifts from friends and family OR the sum total of all those presents as cash?

WOULD YOU RATHER:
Be given a magic 8 ball that is right 75% of the time OR a crystal ball that can show you 5 minutes into the future?

WOULD YOU RATHER:
Be given a voucher for toe enlargement surgery OR finger reduction surgery as a present?

WOULD YOU RATHER:
Be given a mirror that shows you what you looked like yesterday OR a diary that will only show you what you are doing the day after tomorrow as a present?

WOULD YOU RATHER:
Be given cookery classes to prepare a green salad OR Mandarin classes to count from 7 – 23 as a present?

WOULD YOU RATHER:
Be given passwords to every person's social media accounts OR a key that opens the door to every door as a present?

WOULD YOU RATHER:
Be given a life size waxwork model of
Donald Trump OR a stuffed donkey as a
present?

WOULD YOU RATHER:
Be given a chicken that can tell if people are lying by pecking their face OR a giraffe that can read people's minds by licking their ears as a present?

WOULD YOU RATHER:
Be given a lifetime supply of green leather
trousers OR rainbow coloured velour
tracksuits as a present?

WOULD YOU RATHER:
Be given a jam jar full of a stranger's belly button fluff OR earwax as a present?

WOULD YOU RATHER:
Be given a jumper made from used plasters
OR a beanie made from armpit hair as a
present?

WOULD YOU RATHER:
Be given a ring that makes you invisible OR a
watch that stops time as a present?

WOULD YOU RATHER:
Be given your height in Jaffa cakes OR your
weight in cheese as a present?

WOULD YOU RATHER:
Be given a Ferrari OR a helicopter as a present?

WOULD YOU RATHER:
Be given a massage from Donald Trump OR
a rabid koala as a present?

WOULD YOU RATHER:
Be given a lifetime supply of salad cream OR
honey mustard dressing as a present?

WOULD YOU RATHER:
Be given a baby grizzly bear OR a lion cub as a present?

WOULD YOU RATHER:
Be given Captain America's shield OR Thor's hammer as a present?

WOULD YOU RATHER:
Ask for a puppy for Christmas but receive an
African snail OR ask for a kitten and receive
a stick insect?

WOULD YOU RATHER:
Wear underwear made from Reindeer fur OR tinsel?

WOULD YOU RATHER:
Have tinsel for hair OR fairy lights for fingernails?

WOULD YOU RATHER:
Have a nose like Rudolf OR ear's like an elf?

WOULD YOU RATHER:
Have a Santa beard OR reindeer antlers?

WOULD YOU RATHER:
Sneeze tinsel OR poop baubles?

WOULD YOU RATHER:
Go to work/school dressed in a snowman OR reindeer onesie?

WOULD YOU RATHER:
Have sausages wrapped in bacon for toes OR
brussel sprouts for eyes?

WOULD YOU RATHER:
Meet the Prime Minister/President wearing a
festive jumper made from party hats OR
Christmas tree pine needles?

WOULD YOU RATHER:
Have the body of a reindeer OR the face of a snowman?

WOULD YOU RATHER:
For a whole year wear a Christmas party hat
OR a novelty reindeer jumper?

WOULD YOU RATHER:
Wear a Santa suit for all of Christmas OR
have all your regular clothes covered in
jingly bells?

WOULD YOU RATHER:
Meet the Queen wearing a tie made of tinsel
OR a suit jacket made of jazzy wrapping
paper?

WOULD YOU RATHER:
Wake up on Christmas day and discover
your family has been transformed into
Snowmen OR Reindeer?

WOULD YOU RATHER:
Wake up on Christmas day looking like the Grinch OR Jack Skellington (Nightmare before Christmas)?

WOULD YOU RATHER:
Wake up on Christmas day and find yourself
as McCauley Culkin "Home alone"
defending your house against incompetent
burglars OR as a Muppet extra in a Muppet's
Christmas Carol?

WOULD YOU RATHER:
Wake up on Christmas day and find yourself
as a turkey OR a Christmas cracker?

WOULD YOU RATHER:
Wake up on Christmas day and find yourself as The Queen OR The President of the United States of America?

WOULD YOU RATHER:
Wake up on Christmas day and find yourself
as a star OR angel at the top of a Christmas
tree?

WOULD YOU RATHER:
Wake up on Christmas Eve and find yourself
as Santa Claus OR Rudolph?

WOULD YOU RATHER:
Have to sing Christmas carols every time you walk into a room OR wear a Snowman onesie to work/school for a week?

WOULD YOU RATHER:
Spend a day untangling Christmas tree lights
OR listening to the same Christmas carol on
repeat?

WOULD YOU RATHER:
Decorate your Christmas tree with taxidermy spiders OR rats?

WOULD YOU RATHER:
Never hear any Christmas music OR hear the
same three songs all season?

WOULD YOU RATHER:
Not be able to celebrate Christmas OR your birthday?

WOULD YOU RATHER:
Have all your presents encased in trifle OR Christmas pudding?

WOULD YOU RATHER:
Reach into your Christmas stocking and find
a dead mouse OR an alive one?

WOULD YOU RATHER:
Spend Christmas with your family OR a host of celebrities?

WOULD YOU RATHER:
For a whole year only be able to read books
of Christmas cracker jokes OR listen to
Christmas music?

WOULD YOU RATHER:
Travel around by Reindeer OR on a chair
carried by elves?

WOULD YOU RATHER:
Have Christmas in a warm sunny climate OR in a cold snowy climate?

WOULD YOU RATHER:
Come home and find everything you own
wrapped in Christmas paper OR every
surface in your house covered in glitter?

WOULD YOU RATHER:
Spend Christmas on your own OR with the inmates of a maximum security prison?

WOULD YOU RATHER:
Have everything you touch turn to mince
pies OR sausages wrapped in bacon?

WOULD YOU RATHER:
Wrap 100 awkwardly shaped presents OR peel all the veg for a Christmas dinner for 100 people?

WOULD YOU RATHER:
Spill a jug of gravy on a family member OR
tell all your dinner guests your most
embarrassing secret?

WOULD YOU RATHER:
Wake up and every day is Christmas Day OR your Birthday?

WOULD YOU RATHER:
Share Christmas dinner with someone who
spits when they talk OR someone that steals
food from your plate?

WOULD YOU RATHER:
Have to go hunting for your turkey for
Christmas dinner OR just eat a bowl of
Brussel sprouts?

WOULD YOU RATHER:
Celebrate Christmas in house without a
Christmas tree OR have no advent calendar?

Printed in Great Britain
by Amazon